# Tree

*Dianne Robbins*
*and the Tree People*

ISBN  978-0-9849254-6-9 / 0-9849254-6-5  Paperback
978-0-9849254-5-2 / 0-9849254-5-7  E-Book


Images used under license from Shutterstock.com


Printed in the United States of America

Books by Dianne Robbins:

*The Call Goes Out from the Cetacean Nation*

*TELOS: Original Transmissions from the
Subterranean City beneath Mt. Shasta*

*Messages from the Crystal Kingdom*

*Messages from the Hollow Earth*

*Tree Talk*

www.DianneRobbins.com
TelosMtShasta@gmail.com
585-802-4530

# *Dedication*

In deepest Love and Gratitude,
I dedicate this book to the Nature Kingdom.

# *In Appreciation*

To Lawrence M. Frank for supporting
the publication of this book.

**TREE**

**T**aking

**R**esponsibility for the

**E**arth and the

**E**nvironment

# Contents

# *A Note from the Author to "Hug a Tree"*

Our Dear Readers,

Just as the Cetaceans are the Earth's Record Keepers living in the Oceans, do you know that the TREES are the Record Keepers living on Land?

The Trees comprise a "vast underground communication network" system that transmits information so that all Trees, everywhere on Earth, know instantly all that occurs. They are Living Libraries embodied in bark that we, as humans, can easily "tap" into (note the term "tap root"—we can tap into their vast library). Their "line" is always open to us, so tap into it—they are eagerly awaiting our call. They are waiting for us to acknowledge them as the *Tree People.*

For uncensored worldwide news and answers to any question, Hug a Tree—it not only saves paper, but their lives as well.

# How the Tree People Manifested this Book

*In early 2008, Dianne Robbins received this message during a time of meditation:*

We are the 𝒯𝓇𝑒𝑒 𝒫𝑒𝑜𝓅𝓁𝑒, and we would like to begin our dictations to you again. Now that your other book is finished *(The Call Goes Out from the Cetacean Nation),* the way is clear. We, too, need a voice to speak through, and we have chosen you, who have also chosen us. We wave our leaves at you to begin.

We thank you for putting our message on the last page of the Cetacean Nation book. The Cetacean Kingdom has made their voices known through you, and it is now time for the Trees to do the same. We wish you a bon voyage through our leaves that wave in the wind.

# *Foreword from the Tree People*

Greetings, Dear People of Earth. We are the *Tree People,* and we thank you for reading our book of messages, dictated from us to you, for the purpose of acquainting you with our world and seeing the world around you through our eyes. For our eyes encompass all realms, including yours.

As you read our messages of love, know that our love for humanity is deep and profound, for you are the Caretakers of the Earth, and this is your domain. This is your world to love and to cherish. We only remind you of the great responsibility you have, so that you can fulfill it.

Many have come before you, without the awareness of the inter-connectiveness of all life. We only bring this to your attention so that you can see the link between us, yourself, and all life-forms, and care for all of nature's creatures as your own. For indeed, all creatures are your children, whether born of you or not. For there is only one great Mother, and she is the Earth herself—giving birth to us all and giving us all a home to enable us to have the experiences we need for our souls to grow and thrive, so we can move on to higher realms.

So cherish the Earth, feel the sacredness of all life, and walk in harmony as your feet touch the Earth and your heart intertwines with ours.

We thank you for reading our book, and through our messages may you understand the **Great Laws of Life,** and act to bring peace and harmony back to our planet. We stand with you as ONE.

# Trees are Living Libraries

## By Mikos, an Inner Earth Resident

Our Dear Readers: I am *Mikos*, introducing you to the *Tree People* living among you.

The *Tree People* are very Lighted Beings, and you can see how their auras fill the sky in towers of light waves radiating from their inner essences. They are tubes of light, carrying vast amounts of information and folklore to disseminate to humans on Earth, if only humans would tune into their frequency and connect with them on their wavelength. This is easy to do. You just call on the Trees and invoke their presence, and ask them to transfer their library to your vast vault inside yourself. Your vault is practically empty, so you have much storage room inside, just waiting to be filled with documents containing the mysteries of life—all the mysteries you haven't as yet been able to unravel in your closed states of existence.

The Trees are "open" to all, and not closed in their belief systems or ways of thinking. They are open to the Universe and to all life around them, and welcome information coming in from all sources and all places.

They have a cataloging system built right into them that filters and sorts all the information into categories, and then files these categories away for easy retrieval—just like in the most modern of your libraries—only the Trees do it themselves, automatically, without any help from manmade technology. Yes, the Trees are most magnificent Beings, just waiting for you to retrieve all the information and knowledge of the Earth that they have stored over the millennia for you.

Between the Trees and the Cetaceans, you humans have more knowledge at your fingertips than you could ever read through, so we suggest you don't read it—just imbibe it in your souls and it will filter up to you just when you need it. It is that easy. Information at your fingertips—and no need to read your books anymore, unless you want to read them just for the pure enjoyment; but books are not really necessary, for all the stories of the Earth and the Universe are already written and bound

and found in the library rooms inside the Trees—just waiting for you to check them out. They will even give you a library card—encoded with your very own DNA library number on it, so that you can check out information anytime you desire—and there is no need to return it when you are done reading the records—you just keep it stored within you for future use, to retrieve when necessary. Such an easy system—isn't it? Way beyond anything your technology could dream up.

Only the Creator can dream systems like this, so we suggest

you tap into it and start retrieving all the information that is just waiting for you to check out and use for your survival. For survival is now the point where Earth Humans are in their evolution, and you need the information to survive these times of impending cataclysms. This information is crucial for you to have, for it can change the world in an instant by giving you the understanding you need to avert dire possibilities looming on the horizon caused by mankind's ignorance and gross misdeeds.

So tune into the Trees, and also the Cetaceans, for the guidance, information, and training you need to continue your life as a species dedicated to the Earth and not warring with the Earth. For the Earth is not at war—it is only humans who are at war with themselves, taking it out on others who they see as separate from themselves, rather than part of themselves. It is only your closed vision that keeps you in slavery—so reach out to the Trees who will open your eyesight to the gateway leading to the Stars. All you need to see clearly is just a "blink" away.

I am *Mikos*, your fellow traveler to the Stars. We bid you to travel with us—it is not a rocky road as you perceive it, but a well paved and smooth highway if you but connect to all the other life forms who are waving to you to join them along the road to unity with all. For it is in unity that we thrive, whereas in separateness we dive. So lift with us in consciousness, for all Earth is about to embark on a trip of great heights leading to the Stars. You call it "ascension"; we call it time travel leading to other time zones and dimensions, way beyond your current comprehension.

So open your doors to the **Living Libraries** all around you, and take advantage of their accumulation and wealth of knowledge that you so desperately need in your lives, so that you can fulfill your missions here on Earth in ease and grace. It is all waiting for you to plug into—and oh, so easy to do. Just intend it, and it is so. Intention is always the first step, and then consciously connecting and communing with the Trees is the second step, and walking among them, touching them, sitting with them is the third step, and voila, it will happen—you will be privy to their information and will find yourselves able to tap into their vast storage system with no effort—**the words and thoughts will just appear to you as if you are reading them from a script on a movie screen.** It is that easy.

So now that you know how to break the code and enter the Trees' library, we will leave you here, as we ourselves walk into the Library of Porthologos for our morning of further enlightenment as we access the vast vaults of knowledge in our own library's retrieval system that we have gleaned from the Stars.

I am *Mikos*, and I bid you a good day.

# *Turn On the Creator Frequency*

We are the *Nature Kingdom*. You have been on a long journey, learning lessons of life in a limited "consciousness construct". This is why humanity is struggling for survival. Survival is equated with consciousness. The higher the level of consciousness, the less struggle for survival. It's this limited range of consciousness that prevents soul growth from occurring.

Your governments are instrumental in preventing you from experiencing the range of Light Encoded Information that's streaming onto the planet. They do this by manipulating your environment through cell towers, cell phones, TV mind programming, food, water, and the air you breathe. It's a campaign to thwart your growth and turn you into a robot, and they are succeeding on a mass scale. The best remedy for this is your return to Nature.

So turn off their frequency by going out into Nature where you can **turn on the Creator Frequency,** and you will by-pass the darkness and re-bound into the Light. You can consciously do this through your awareness. We will help you.

# *Trees are the Stewards of the Land*

## *By Mikos*

The Trees are Majestic Beings, evolved beyond anything your thoughts can picture. They wait for you to recognize them also as the stewards of the land, as the Cetaceans are the stewards of the sea, always giving you the oxygen you need, and absorbing the pollutants you create. And what do

you do in return for this gift of life? You cut them down, you move them out of your way, and you ignore them. They are yearning to communicate with you, yearning to feel your touch and embrace you in their love and energy.

Go to them, talk to them, sit with them, as they stand vigilant over your homes and communities as protectors of your very lives. Talk to them, and they will answer. They have been waiting eons to have humans reconnect to them again.

(Excerpted from *Messages from the Hollow Earth,* by Dianne Robbins)

# Prana in the Oceans
# is the Staff of Life

## By Corky, an Orca Whale

Corky is here. It is the Ocean that supplies the Life Force that keeps our Whale bodies and spirits alive. You on land lack this Life Force, as you've polluted your air and soil and water. The Oceans are the last untouched reaches, where it is still possible to swim in the pure Prana that keeps all life alive, and it is Prana that we Orcas breathe. **It is Prana that Trees and Plants consume, that keep them alive regardless of the soil condition or pollution of the air. Trees and Plants get their nutrients directly from the God Source instead of relying on the soil and air.** Prana is invisible to the eye, yet denser than molecules. It is pure food, in the perfect combination that keeps our bodies alive. Yes, we Orcas need our food from fish, but we imbibe Prana also—as it is our "Staff of Life".

(From *The Call Goes Out from the Cetacean Nation,* by Dianne Robbins)

# We Trees Long for
# Physical Contact with You

We are the *Tree People,* all decked out in our summer greenery ready to burst forth into song and spread our melodies far and wide over the countryside. It is a joy to experience summer, and we are now at the height of the solstice, the apex of the demarcation of the seasons, ready to dig into the Earth for this growing season where we grow rapidly after sitting dormant all the winter months. All life experiences these bursts of growth in the summer seasons, and all life longs for the hot sun.

Our talk today will be about you—our human brothers and sisters situated next to us on the surface—and yet you hardly see or recognize us as we stand before you in all our glory. We stand here as sentinels, just waiting for you to pay attention to us—to talk to us—to touch us and wrap your arms around our trunks as far as you can reach. We long for this physical contact with you—this hands-on contact where we can embrace each other at long last. For our branches reach out to you to touch, and our leaves fall to the ground for you to pick up and hold. We are always reaching out to you with our songs that are carried on the wind, if you but tune your ears to listen—for we sing loud and clear, and our melodies are carried far and wide.

We are deeply dug in here, and we are not leaving the Earth plane without humanity coming along. Yes, some of our souls have left their barked bodies—but most of us remain encased in our bark, waiting for the ascension as you do. We have been embodied for so long compared to the short life of humans that we would not deliberately leave now, with such a short time left to go before the ascension waves occur.

We stand firm in our stance, and firm in our resolve to remain here on the surface and ascend with all life forms and Earth herself. We will not abandon our posts. There is too much at stake now, and every one of us is needed…our Light is crucial at this time to create the Light Wave that will propel us into our ascension mode.

If only humans could communicate with all the other life forms, you would know what is occurring on the Earth and you would be better able to prepare yourselves for the changes that are fast coming. Knowledge is what has been kept from you, keeping you in ignorance of life around you.

We are here to help you understand life, if you would but take the time and give us your attention and tap into our vast library system of daily occurrences…just one day of communicating with us would give you the direction you need to set your life back on course and give you the knowledge you need to understand what is happening and to prepare yourselves for what is about to occur planet-wide. So we stand here, waiting for you to acknowledge us and to tap into our hearts for a Tree Connection—our line is always open, and it is free.

# *Connecting with the Elementals*

We are the *Elementals*, here with you as you sit at your computer. We are perched all around you, as you have been calling and communing with us. We will work with you too, and we will give you our messages. Our messages can be interspersed with the *Tree People's* messages. We can begin now.

We are the Elemental Kingdom, and wish to also be part of this book. We are here in your domain, as prevalent as you are. There are so many of us here now, that we overflow your surroundings and accompany you on all your walks in Nature. We are here to work with you as co-creators and in partnership. This is how both our races evolve. We must work together as

One to more rapidly evolve. Your race has been de-volving because you have cut yourselves off from us and from all other life on Earth. **Now is the time to acknowledge our existence and connect with all of us.** There are many different kinds of *Elementals*, and we all wish to work with humans. This is why we are here on Earth—not to work separately, but together with each other. You can understand more of what we are trying to convey to you, by reading Tanis Helliwell's book *Summer with the Leprechauns.* (This is a true story.)

This is the next step in your evolution, to connect with the Trees and now us, the *Elementals*—especially your very own Body Elemental who waits for you to become consciously aware of its existence. We will teach you to manifest and teach you to co-create your dreams. So reach to us, as we reach to you. You will find us wherever you are, but especially out in Nature where it is quiet and serene. We wait for you there. Good day.

# We Trees are Record Keepers

We are the Trees. We, too, are Record Keepers. Our branches are layered with information. Our leaves are recording plates that capture your words and actions as you walk by. You can talk to us and we will record your words, even your nuances of speech. It is like turning a dial on a recording device and you talk into it. We are better than that, since we don't run on technology—it is built into us.

Our leaves look thin to your eyes, yet hold volumes of information that appears automatically to you in vision and sound when you "switch on" to us. We are self-contained books holding the records of the Earth. As our leaves sway to and fro in the wind we are sweeping the ethers and picking up pertinent information that is necessary to sustain life. It is all encoded and you can easily break the code. We can answer any question you ask if you just learn to hear us. We speak loud and clear to your heart—not your ear.

We Trees comprise a vast underground communications network that records all events and is privy to all that is about to occur. If you want to know what is going to happen anywhere on Earth, just stand next to one of us and put your hand on our trunk and ask your question. We will answer.

We Trees are guardians—sentinels stationed on Earth to serve here along with you in partnership as caretakers. We are encoded with cosmic intelligence and graced by the Divine just as you are—only we are aware of our gifts and use them to create only harmony.

You can read us as we read you—you are a Living Library

and can turn the pages within your soul to access all there is to know. It is built into you…it is you. This is why your DNA is so sought after and you have been so tampered with. You are a prize worth capturing but no one can duplicate you. With all their technology they still cannot figure you out. Only the Creator knows the code.

# We Invite You Into Our
# Mt. Shasta Woodland Homes

Greetings from under the shade of our branches. We were all united with you when you were in our Mountain home atop Mt. Shasta in California. Our leaves and boughs caressed you and our auras merged with yours. We thank you for visiting us on the mountain, and wait for you to return. Our hearts are filled with love for you and our connection was profound. So do come again—often—for this location is one of great mystery, and your presence will unravel its secrets. We wait for you.

Greetings from the Tree World. We are the *Tree People,* so happy to be united with you again, or shall we say reunited! Our love for humanity is great, and it is this love that we wish to have returned to us, to complete the circle of life—for all our lives are greatly affected by the amount of love we emit and send to others. It is what keeps us all alive…from the newborn to the elderly…although there are no elderly among us…only immortal souls living out this Earth experience to gain more wisdom and to improve our quality of life. This quality of life is what is in question for humanity now, for without quality, why even have life? It detracts from the purpose, doesn't it?

We all came here to improve the quality of life and to improve the quality of experiences we chose to have, and to experience life on a higher level, but humanity doesn't seem to understand this—instead you are creating experiences that take you further away from Source, instead of bringing you closer to Source. Moving closer to Source is why we came here. We came here to use our experiences to move our consciousness closer to Source, so that some day in the eternal future, we can become creators and create planets and solar systems ourselves; because as a result of our living experiences here on Earth we would have learned the eternal Universal Laws governing Nature. It is these Laws we came here to learn, and we use our experiences with each other to learn them. Using each other is the way to learn, because these laws are not found in your books—your books contain only dead pages devoid of the life force needed to learn from. Our lives contain the life force and our experiences are propelled by the life force, and it is this life force that brings us the experiences we need for our soul growth. So journey with us on this path, so that your souls can expand and learn the lessons you need to continue on your evolutionary path leading to your ascension. There is no time to lose.

## The Elementals Speak

Yes, we would like to talk about this too, and add our wisdom to the brew. We, too, were gathered all around you when you were on our Mountain, and we were singing to you in our softest voices—our voices connecting directly to your hearts. You did hear us, but on a higher level out of your auditory reach. Our voices carry on the wind on a higher frequency than your hearing range can pick up. But just because you cannot hear us, does not mean we did not sing back to you. You did hear our words, "Sing to us and we will sing back to you"…and this we did. Know that what you ask from us will come to you—always—even though you may not yet be able to perceive it with your physical senses. But the time is fast approaching when you will be able to perceive all around you—you will be able to tap into our magical world and experience the magic of existence that we live daily.

We honor you for making this connection to us in our home on the Mountain…for it is your home too…all prepared for your visits to us. It was nice and comfy, wasn't it? And so serene. This is our living space, and our environment is always in peace. We experience only serenity—except when loggers and noisy people encroach upon our space and disturb us with their discordant energies. Otherwise we can evolve rapidly in our consciousness because we have the environment to do so.

Your living environment is not conducive to life. It is that simple. Life is not meant to be lived in noise. Everything in your lives is now inundated with noise. Wherever you go, discordant sound, which you call music, is played to disrupt your thoughts so that you cannot even think through a thought anymore without being distracted. This is everywhere—from gas stations to restaurants to airplanes, and now people even play "music" outside their stores to lure people in. Well, if you cannot think, you will think you need to buy everything when you hear the music. The music is to deaden your senses so that you can become random buyers to support the "system" that is robbing you of your life—to make you think that life is about buying things camouflaged against a background of "music". Well, this "music" is programmed to take your free will choices away from you, and make you slaves to the establishment.

You keep buying your way deeper and deeper into slavery and debt; making malls your aphrodisiacs instead of Nature. It is Nature that will cure all, and restore your senses and bring you the emotional balance your soul cries for. Malls are dead zones. Nature is a live zone. Do you see the difference? Well, you really cannot see it, you have to go out in Nature and then you will assuredly feel it. So come outdoors to us, and we will put you back on track so that you can raise your awareness and contribute to life, not destroy it.

We don't know how to reach you…your senses seem so deadened and your hearts so hard from the struggles of life. All we can do is invite you into our woodland homes and surround you with our love. Our gentleness and songs will sooth you, and as you relax into our embrace you will begin to feel our presence and this will begin our merging. There is no other way. **You must come to us, so that we can come to you.** It is so easy to do, and you will feel so good. So why wait?

Our love for you is strong, for we know you as ourselves. We know all life forms as ourselves. It is this that you have to know, and you can only know it from being with us. You cannot learn it from a book—you can only learn it from our **living Presence** that is all around you. We are so close to you—we surround your homes, so step outside and touch us, sit under us, and talk to us. We will all crowd around you when you are outdoors, and you will feel heaven within. For it is our "heavenly" vibration we bring to you to offset the lower vibration of your lives. So the more you are with us, the higher your vibration climbs, until you are once again merged wholly with Source and back on your evolutionary path through the Stars.

We thank you for merging your heart with ours, and taking our messages. We are truly One and can feel it deeply inside as we impart this feeling back to you.

We are the *Elementals* conjoined with the Trees. We wish you a good day of laughter and cheer.

*You came to experience ALL THAT IS.*

*You came to be a part of the*
*Transformation and Regeneration*
*of all life into LIGHT.*

*You came to help*
*and you came to learn.*

*You are Great LIGHTBEARERS.*

Love Notes
from
Dianne's Trees

# *I Am Your Tree*

My roots go deep into the ground.
I love you.

My energy and strength is for you to take
whenever you need it.
Just call to me and ask to receive it
and I will direct the flow of my strength into your body.

I live and breathe the Earth, just as you do.
I am stationary, but my thoughts travel far.
I am in communication with all Trees on Earth.
We live to give life to humans—we live for all life forms
that they may evolve amidst beauty and strength.

# My Tree in My Classroom

This is your Tree. I am totally connected to all the other Trees through my consciousness. Although my roots don't tap into the Earth, my consciousness still flows out from my branches. My roots are trapped in this container, but my consciousness is free. Thank you for keeping me so close to you in your room. We are One.

# All Creation Fits Into One Classroom

I stand silently and vigilant, and watch over you daily. You are a shining star and your light merges with mine at night. We light up the sky. All consciousness is One, and as you move higher on the spectrum of Light, so do I and all beneath us. We all travel together as One.

We, too, meet on the Inner Planes at night, and attend the same classes—as all Creation attends night school in whatever form they are in. Remember, Consciousness is One. I don't take up that much space on the Inner Planes—we all fit into the room where the lecture is given. All of creation can fit into one classroom. You are surprised? Yet this is true.

Best wishes on your Journey in Consciousness. May you discover all the intricacies of the Universe and know that we are One. See you tonight. I love you. Your Tree.

# *We Trees Stand in Our Divinity*

*From Dianne's Tree in her backyard*

I am your Tree. Thank you for sitting under my wings. Thank you for napping within my embrace. I, too, can fly! Although my trunk remains dug in, my consciousness soars to other places and even to other Star Systems. For we Trees are very evolved also, just incarnated in a different "stationary" form to "oversee" the land.

This is why we have "height"—so that we can see far and wide over the countryside. We know what is happening around you at every moment. Even though you are moving around, you are not able to perceive the movement around you, as you have dulled your senses and perceptions through pollution and doubt. You have not claimed your divinity and this prevents you from recognizing all the varied life forms around you.

We Trees stand in our divinity and mirror our divineness to you—if you could but see and feel our branches reaching out to touch you as you walk by. So stop for a moment. Take time from your hectic pace and touch us—hold us—sit under us—and we will respond by invigorating and rejuvenating you with our energy—for supply is endless, as is our love for you. I am your Tree and you are me.

*(left) This is "My Tree" in my backyard who channels messages to me, and when I sit under her branches, she becomes an extension of me, and is my antenna to the stars.*

45

# We Trees are the Ground Crew

I am your Tree. Thank you for being here with me, as I am ever here for you. I wait patiently outdoors, beside your window, waiting for you to acknowledge and think of me. Your time under my boughs is very precious to me, for it gives me the time to commune directly with you as your body is within my range of frequency and your proximity is within my immediate location.

We are both old souls from the past, here again to bring in and anchor Light from our Father's abode on high. We serve together again, as we did in our past incarnations, to continue to give Light to humanity's developing souls, so they may cease wars and begin to live in the peace that was meant to be.

We Trees are here in service to the Galactic Command too—only we are the "ground crew" who have "dug in" and live in our "dug outs" so to speak, while doing the same job and having the same assignment as you, who walk on foot and travel on land. It's just that our "physicality" is stationed in one spot, while our leaves blow hither and yon in the wind, and our scent and voices travel far inland. For we communicate with all life on the surface and below the surface, just as you do.

Our boughs reach through many dimensions, as we stand guard on Earth, and we are privy to information coming in on different wave bands also. Our auras are vast, and connect us to one another across space, and we span Earth's globe and hold her tightly within our auric arms of green and gold. We bless the Earth, for she has given us life—life to reveal our innermost natures and life to express ourselves in so many myriad ways and forms. **For as you walk, we talk, and our voices ever follow your footsteps,** guiding you on your path through Nature's inner-most realms where you can play and experience the magic of our species, albeit in different form.

When you are with us, you are also with the Deva Spirits who are the Stewards of your yard. They, too, wish to correspond with you:

## The Deva Spirits Speak

We are your Deva brothers and sisters. We work with your grass and flowers in your back yard, and we love your company—we love it when you sit outdoors and commune with us. For even though our species differs greatly from yours, our consciousness is still One. Therefore, we can always read your thoughts when they are centered on us.

When you sleep under your Tree, we are all there surrounding and protecting your body as you travel in space. We are here for you, and ever shall be. We love you, our dearest sister on Earth. The Deva Spirits.

# *Tree Guides*

We Trees are also Guides, and we guide you unerringly through the brambles and snares in your lives. Our roots go down deep and we can guide you through the tangles you have woven in your lives, and back up to sunlit clarity.

Our roots go down deep, so deep that etherically they actually penetrate through the Earth and come out on the other side hearing and knowing and bringing all information with us in our journeys as we sweep through Earth's depths.

Our roots are privy to all that is occurring and we communicate it to all. Our reception is clear, and never interfered with. We are so grounded in our stance that nothing can sway us except for your bulldozers and logging equipment; otherwise, we hold the ground firmly and balance the Earth as it wobbles on its trajectory through space. If all humans were balanced, there would be no wobble. Although we are stationary, we travel constantly and have more freedom of movement than you.

# *We are the Trees on Mt. Shasta*

Come to the Mountain
Walk on the stones
Hold on to our branches
You are not alone

We are more than a speck
We are pebbles that are blessed
Our light shines through stones
We are your home

As you walk on us
You feel our touch
We caress your feet
With our love soft and sweet

The breezes caress you
The winds touch your skin
Our love is all around you
We beckon you in

To our vibration
Where we are stationed
To monitor the Earth
Through mounds of dirt

Which isn't just dirt
But consciousness alive
Touching all who walk upon us
To make your bodies thrive

We are more than a speck
We are consciousness at rest
Any stress
Is only a test

So come to the Mountain
We beckon you in
The Faeries will greet you
You will feel them within

It's never dark
Our light is bright
It shines through the ethers
To lovingly greet you

Night isn't night
Day isn't day
It is all the same
It is you who light the way

You light up the Mountain
You light up the Earth
You light up the Cosmos
As a result of your birth

We need you on Earth
We need you here
So don't be afraid
You are part of us, my dear

# *Pluck It When It Appears*

We are the Trees. There is much that you do not know about us or the *Weather People* called the *Elementals*. We are always pushing away the debris and pollutants that cloud your vision, but you too must push away your negative thoughts and despair and see the love that is coming through to you each and every moment. Yes, things may not be working out in your personal lives as you would wish them to, but look at them as stepping stones into the next phase of your evolutionary spiral where more of what you desire is just waiting to be plucked.

**But the key is to pluck it when it appears, or it disappears back into the ethers. You must also be clear in your calls, and intend the specifics of your desires. Your dreams will materialize quickly now, so hold only hope in your heart.**

You are the knowingness
to your questions.

As you reach ever higher
in your divine consciousness
you will access all you need to know,
when you need it.

It is all stored there for you,
Ready to fill your mind and heart
with the answers you seek.

# Caring for
# Our Common Home

# *We are Your Inbreath*

Greetings. We are the *Tree People,* standing watch over you as you type our message.

We sing to you of times to come when the whole Earth's surface will be free of tyranny, and when our people will be able to stand in freedom along with yours, without the fear of being trampled, burned or cut down.

We know that you, too, are in need of space to live on, just as we need more space for our communities to spread our roots and branches out in, for we, too, are cramped in our living space as more and more of us are being cut down to make room for your malls and housing projects and grazing lands. We are also ripped out of the ground so that miners can mine the minerals in the Earth, with no regard to our habitats. Yes, we Trees have habitats also. The land is our habitat, and we don't like to be encroached upon either, or cut down to get us out of your way so that you can drill into the Earth's body to remove her life sustenance.

There is no difference between us and other life forms. We all need our own habitats to live in, and without enough space and protection we cannot thrive. We live in trepidation of being harmed and maimed and cut down just as other life forms feel when their habitats are threatened and are purposely destroyed so that humans can spread out without any regard for others who also share our great Earth's body.

This is a travesty of Nature. But humans are waking up and realizing that all of Nature is part of Creation, and all of Nature means all of you, too. There is no separation between any of us. This will become more and more apparent to the masses as your governments continue to destroy the very home you live on. You will finally be able to make the connection between the Earth's well-being and your well-being. You cannot live without us.

**We give you the oxygen to breathe and you give us the carbon dioxide we need to breathe—it is a complete cycle of living energy—we are your inbreath, and your outbreath gives us our inbreath—if one of us becomes extinct, the other immediately follows.** This is the cycle of life that all are dependent on. We all need each other to live, and you are just now discovering this dependency. All species are part of this great life cycle, and all are needed to keep it perfectly functioning. It is the great rhythm of life that we all carry out together. Every single species, every single plant, every stone contributes to the overall plan of Creation, and without each and every one of us, life will eventually collapse, as part of the biosphere collapses each time a species is lost through extinction due to mankind's wars and intrusions into our sacred habitats.

Do you understand this? Now, you ask, "What can I, one person, do?" Well, we will give you the answer. You can stop stepping on flowers when you walk, or picking them for your tables. You can revere the beauty of the landscape instead of destroying it. You can protect our habitats by standing by our side when your bulldozers come to our home to cut us down. You can stand up to them, just as you would stand up to protect your children if harm were coming their way or if someone were coming into your house to take them away. We are your family too—do you not remember this? We remind you that

all life is part of the Great Family of Creation, and we are all related in ways you cannot yet imagine. We are related through the great life force of the Creator—we are related through our Souls! Yes, our souls are all One Soul, just dressed in different clothing so that we can complete the circle of life necessary for life to thrive on Earth. We each give and take from each other, so that we all have all that we need. But we don't take each other's lives. We just exchange our gifts of life that we are born with in order to sustain each other. It is the circle of life and you are part of it, not separate from it.

So join with us now, before it is too late. Together we are one great bastion of strength, and our unity is a barrier that cannot be penetrated. We are the Light, and together we can outshine the darkness. But we must stand together, and not let anyone or anything divide us.

You keep your family together don't you? You don't let

anyone remove your children from your home, do you? Well, we are your family, so don't let anyone remove us from our home—which is this whole Earth. **None of us should be removed from any of our homes for any reason.** Wherever we are planted is our home—whether it is in a house, a forest or in the Ocean. This is our home, and **trespassing is not part of the Divine Plan of Creation.**

We Trees don't come into your houses and take your children do we? Well, don't come into our communities and take us for firewood. There is abundant free energy everywhere that is just waiting to be tapped. You don't need our bodies to light your fires, and we certainly don't need your bodies to give us warmth. We provide our own. In fact, the Earth provides all that we could ever need for our growth and comfort, except for the carbon dioxide you breathe to us.

The same applies to you. Your bodies were originally equipped with all the internal mechanisms you need to keep you warm in the winters and cool in the summers. But you lost this mechanism of innate internal regulation as you became more and more used to your city living instead of living on the land out in Nature. You lost your connection to Nature, which is your connection to yourself. **Your bodies were meant to self-regulate your internal temperature to keep you warm in the winter and cool in the summer, so that you could live outdoors all year long.** Do you know this? The book series "The Ringing Cedar Series" is a living example of what we are talking about. (Book 1 is *Anastasia* by Vladimir Megre, Ringing Cedars Press, www.RingingCedars.com)

God, in all his perfection, also made you in all your perfec-

tion, but your ways of living have detracted from your perfection and your DNA has been tampered with by the dark forces who have been trying to control your evolution and slow it down to a snail's pace.

Knowing who you are is crucial to your evolution and to your rise in consciousness. Once you know who you are, you become a force that no-one will meddle with, for you then stand in the power of your great I AM PRESENCE.

All life forms on Earth are beckoning you to join with them as One Mighty Force of Creation—capable of overcoming all that is not of the Light. So join with us now, before it is too late.

We are the *Tree People.* Good day.

# Q: Are you managing Nature in the Hollow Earth, or do you leave it untouched?

## Answered by Mikos

We always leave Nature herself untouched, as she is the best doctor there is, to solve her own problems without our interference. She has been doing this since life on Earth began, and who are we to step in and interfere? She has all the innate knowledge within her DNA, and can administer all the remedies her trees and plants and flowers need, in perfect dosages.

Letting Nature cure herself is the best remedy of all. We find that all our trees and plants and flowers in the Inner Earth and in Telos are always in perfect health, perfect shape, and perfectly glorious. We never tamper with what Nature creates, and this is the secret. This is why you have so many problems growing your food, plants, and trees on the surface, because you are continually interfering with Nature's plan that has been perfected by the Creator in advance of your inhabiting the Earth's surface.

Look how your soil has become depleted of nutrients, your rainforests cut down, your air and waterways polluted, all contributing to the disease and decay of your flora and fauna, including human life. When will you learn to honor and respect Mother Nature as the great Goddess she truly is? She knows so much more than your tree doctors, plant doctors, and animal doctors. She knows exactly what each life form needs for a healthy and happy life, and she provides it all bountifully—and if you just leave her alone, she will rebuild herself faster than the wink of an eye. The health of all trees can be restored within your lifetime, which is very quick indeed, considering that it took millions of years to evolve into the glorious forests that only recently once were.

The trees themselves want desperately to stay alive and participate in Earth's ascension plan. But isn't it strange that surface folk never consider them as part of Earth's life forms, nor ask their permission to cut them down? The trees never asked to be part of your wars, yet are maimed and killed where they stand as sentinels in war zones—body counts are not taken for trees, yet they are another war casualty in a different life form who never volunteered nor gave consent to be part of man's war crimes to plunder the Earth for her oil reserves and destroy whole countries in the process.

People never consider that the trees are here to evolve too, and to ascend along with humans. All life forms are on the ascension path, and anything detrimental that we do to retard or destroy their lives puts a block on their ascension path. Theirs is not any different from the path humans take to ascend. We just all do it in different body forms and in different ways.

Here in the Inner Earth we consult with all life forms on all matters that concern the well being of us all. All life forms are represented at our meetings. Our state of existence has been, is, and always will be peaceful.

So you don't need tree doctors, or doctors for anything. Nature has its own inbuilt pharmacy and knows when to dispense its remedies and exactly how much to keep all of us in divine physical perfection. But of course we have to do our part and not pollute Mother Nature with chemtrails, chemicals, biological warfare, or fertilizers, so that she can remain healthy and strong, as life is intended to be. It is just humans who are destroying the perfection of Mother Earth, a Divine Being in herself.

Divinity is always perfect, and divinity always stays perfect. This includes you, the humans who live on the surface. You are made in the Creator's image, and you were made perfect. You still are perfection, if you could only see your divine blueprint that you came into the Earth with and that you still carry in your DNA. It is only you yourself who have marred and changed and distorted and imbalanced yourselves so that your divine blueprint can no longer express the perfection you are, as it was intended to do.

Your doctors are the worst offenders and culprits, prescribing drugs and chemicals that further interfere with your divine blueprint for perfection and drug your senses and jam your frequencies so that you are barely conscious anymore, and mostly asleep, as you sleepwalk through your daily life. This is a great, booming business for your doctors, who are monetarily thriving on your sickness and promote it daily with their advertisements in your media. Big bonuses are given to your doctors for prescribing deadly medications. The pharmaceutical companies are thriving the most, while you suffer the most, just to line their pockets with money as they proclaim their "cures" for the diseases that they create.

Wake up humans; it is your duty to revolt. Your great country, the United States of America, was created from a revolution decrying injustice and tyranny. Well, the same situation has developed again, and it is again the time to revolt to throw off the shackles of tyranny, where corporations and governments of greed dominate and the human people and tree people suffer. Revolution is your birthright. You owe it to your country to revolt—to get rid of the tyrants in your government, corporations, and pharmaceuticals, and to live FREE of coercion and free of disease and pollution. Then all will thrive, in divine, physical perfection.

We step back now, and we thank you for your question. I am *Mikos*.

(Excerpted from *TELOS: Original Transmissions from the Subterranean City beneath Mt. Shasta,* by Dianne Robbins)

# Fires Set Off in California
# is Eco-Terrorism

Greetings, our brothers and sisters dwelling under the shade of our leaves and boughs of our branches. We are the *Tree People,* standing on your land-forms in all our majesty and grace. We sing to you through our branches and leaves, hoping the tune will "catch you" and you will feel our essences and rejoice in our contact. We will talk to you now about the fires in the state of California and the smoke shrouding your Mountain in Mt. Shasta and covering you with soot and ashes and particles unhealthy to breathe.

These fires were targeted and set off by your secret government who is using Nature to burn our lives and pollute the air with our smoke to make you sick so that they can reduce the population through sickness and better control your lives through fear. It is the most "smart" weapon they now have available, with the technology back-engineered from fallen space craft and given to them by the unholy negative extra-terrestrials.

They knew exactly where the lightning strikes would hit, because they themselves precisely targeted the locations and then detonated the lightning charges. It is quite simple, and they have excelled in this kind of warfare, using all the forces of Nature and making it appear as if it is Nature herself who is responsible for this. (The new name for this kind of warfare is **Weather Warfare,** and it is the military's plan to **Draft Mother Nature.** This name is from the book *Weather Warfare,* by Jerry E. Smith.)

Yes, Nature herself is creating some disasters in response to the unequilibrium in her body caused by humanity's total disregard for her life. But, we must say this, that most of these earthquakes, tsunamis, floodings, droughts, volcano eruptions, winds, hurricanes, tornadoes, fires—you name it—are now being deliberately caused by your governments to solve their problem of having too many of you on the surface, because too many people are too hard to control. The less people they have to control, the more they can put you into servitude to themselves—and this is their ultimate goal: to own you and to own the Earth.

We Trees stand here and watch it all unfold. We try to make contact with you, but you turn a deaf ear and blind eye to us, and ignore us as we stand silently right by your very side. We are here as your bastions of strength, your warriors in disguise, who when aligned with you can overthrow the tyranny of these dark ones by our combined strength and wisdom.

All the Forces of Nature are on your side, if you will but align with our consciousness and stand solidly with us to disarm them. We do this through our combined consciousness—for when we combine our consciousness, our Light exponentially magnifies and accelerates at speeds beyond your current imaginations—and the Light when exponentially magnified increases its Light Quotient which can disarm and neutralize and quell all negativity on Earth, leaving not only humanity, but all life forms, free to evolve as we were always meant to.

Do you see why it is so important to connect with us? You have heard of the term "divide and conquer"? Well, this tactic is obvious here in the Nature realm, and the darkness knows this tactic so well. They have divided us by separating us because of our different forms. Well, now you are on to their game, and it is not so difficult to figure it out, is it? Just unite with us, and we can be a force so great that even their best strategists would not know what to do, and would give up in alarm and flee their posts. You know this phrase well: "United we stand, divided we fall."

So stand with us in our strength, and we will carry you to Freedom. All other life forms are connected with us, as we are connected with all, except you humans…who up until now have wanted no part of the rest of God's Creation. But since you are also part of God's Creation, why not join forces with all of us—not just our *Tree People,* but all of Nature's Creations, all of Nature's Life Forms—and lend your consciousness to all of ours, and we will be able to surmount and overcome all tyranny everywhere on Earth.

We invite you, our human brothers and sisters, to be part of the solution, not part of the problem. Separation is part of the problem—actually, separation is the whole problem, and none of this would have occurred had you not separated yourselves from each other and from us. Then you could not have been fooled and deceived, because you would have had access through our combined group consciousness to know the truth of what is happening before it got so out of control. Now your life is controlled, rather than you controlling your life.

We are the *Tree People,* but we speak on behalf of all other life forms stationed on your surface.

We wish you a good day.

# *Your Unending Wars Against Nature*

We are the *Tree People,* also decked out in our Sunday best of greenery, standing tall and firm in the ground. Although there is much smoke surrounding us here in the state of California, we see through the smoke and it doesn't cloud our vision as it clouds yours. We know you cannot see the Mountain from your house or city of Mt. Shasta, but we Trees that surround you can see it.

As you connect more and more to us, you connect more and more to yourself. Connection is the key, and from connecting to us, realms of possibilities open up, taking you into dimensions undreamed of. You connect to us through your heart, and when you do, we immediately feel it and resonate back to you our love, thus completing the circle.

All our lives we've waited for you to acknowledge us, and now it is happening. Our lives are very long compared to yours. We live hundreds and thousands of years if not interfered with, and we remember all that occurs throughout our life. We remember every experience and every passer-by. Our memories are intact, and we never lose them. We communicate with all of Nature, especially the birds who live in our branches and make their homes in our leaves. We are a resting place for them, a place where they can congregate safely and raise their young. Our Trees are home to many species, and most could not live without our presence. We are more than you can conceive. Our lives are so intertwined with all life, that without us, there would be nothing—just barren landscapes devoid of movement like Mars. **Every one of us that you cut down brings you closer and closer to the barrenness of Mars.**

Your lives are now filled with the lushness of our growth and landscape of our flowers, bushes, and stately forms towering above you. As you look at the horizon and over your fields you see only green, interspersed with the colors of flowers, songs of birds, and sounds of the streams. Soon these will all disappear, if you don't wake up now to our existence as Sentient Beings and the need for you to care for and preserve our domains.

We cannot live under these conditions of warfare, where every moment we wonder if we are going to be the next casualty in your unending wars against yourselves and against Nature. We never asked to be part of your wars, yet we have been maimed and killed just like humans. Most humans never asked to be part of your wars either; they were just drawn into them by dint of their geographical location. But soon, there won't be enough space for all of us to live on, if so much of the land is destroyed and marred by droughts and erosion. Even though there isn't a military battle on your land, there is still a battle being fought by the dark forces to deplete your land of nutrients so that your crops don't grow and you can't breathe.

The chemtrails are taking care of this, and instead of military forces bombing your land, the chemtrails are bombing you. These chemtrails are more obscure, and most of you don't recognize them as the culprits killing your land and people, because you don't see them. But they are just as real as the military sending soldiers to wreak havoc on your land. There is no difference. The only difference is, one you can see and recognize, and the other you don't see, or refuse to recognize. But the results are the same...the depletion and insidious destruction of your land, so that you can no longer grow your crops on it, and you have to move off your farms. The same applies to the Tree Farms. We are being sprayed with chemtrails too, against the wishes of the farmers. All the organic crops are being sprayed from above, and this is making all of us ill, and all of the crops are becoming unhealthy to eat.

All of Earth is becoming barren and desolate, and soon will look like Mars. Mars used to be lush and green, with raging

rivers, oceans, and streams before their technology destroyed them. This is what is happening to you—again—you are replaying your lives on Mars. Yes, many of you came from Mars when you destroyed your planet. So here you are doing it again. People, you must rise up and protest this travesty on your homeland and not allow it to continue. Come together and bring your group consciousness into focus and see the Earth covered in green, with clean, clear bodies of water and clean, clear air and bright blue skies where you can see forever.

We Trees are grand indeed, and we know that you are grand Beings also. Only you don't know it, and this is the problem. If you could only see the grandness that each of you are, you would see it in everything and honor everything as a result. So first you must see yourself in all your grandness, and then see all of Nature in the same way. See the Earth as the grand Being that she is, perfect in form with all her life forms lit up, reflecting the Creator in their souls. For the Creator is part of all our souls, from the tiny microbe to the largest Tree. The size does not matter because the substance is the same—God consciousness exists in us all, except for humans who see only themselves as superior to us all, rather than seeing the God in us all. Before you can see the God in us all, you have to see and acknowledge the God in yourself; then you will know that **all of existence is the Creator in form.** This is how the Creator expresses itself—in myriad forms on myriad planets, solar systems, galaxies, and universes.

You are not unique here on Earth, you just think you are because your vision is so limited and your thoughts so confined to your daily struggle of existence. So take some time off from your struggles and give them a "coffee break", and go into the Nature spots in your area and walk among the Trees, but don't step on the flowers—only admire and bless them. Dip your feet into the streams and bask in the sun and lie on the ground, feeling Mother Nature embrace and caress your weary souls—souls who have been traveling lifetime after lifetime in search of enlightenment and completion of your karmic path.

**You can speed up your journey into Light by connecting with us on a soul level, so all our souls can make this journey together in hyper-time, and not at the snail's pace that you have been traveling by trying to do it alone. We are all here together because we are all meant to work together in our common goal of ascending together. But how can we all ascend together if you don't even recognize us as your brothers and sisters who live in different life forms?**

Someday you will all be awakened and find yourselves where your beliefs have taken you. Some will have ascended, and some will remain on a 3rd dimensional sphere, still trying to wake up to who they are. So wake up now—why wait any longer? **All together we can ascend now. Remember, there is no time—so why delay it? It can all be done right now—ascension in any moment can occur when enough humans align with all of the Nature Kingdom.** It is that easy. And all of Nature is ready, including the Elemental Kingdom who watches over you and your bodies, even though you are as yet unaware of them and the great part they play in your evolution. **Your Body Elemental is waiting for you to acknowledge it** and work with it so that you can be the co-creators you came here to be. This is another part of yourself you have yet to become aware of that all the rest of Nature is already consciously working with in a partnership.

My, how you humans have isolated yourselves into individual Beings separated from the rest of life! The human species represents but a tiny speck in all of Creation, and yet you see yourself as the only life form and only intelligent species on the only planet among billions of Universes. How narrow is your perception! As you expand your perception, your vision expands, and you begin to see all of existence in its myriad forms. It is all about "seeing"—and not through your physical eyes, but your inner eyes, where you bring the unseen worlds into yourself, where all of existence lies. It is all within you, not outside you. But if you go outside into Nature, you will find us all within you. And when you find us within, you can out-picture us and meld with our essence. This melding will give you the added strength and clarity that will open your eyes to the Universe that lies within you. This we, the Nature Kingdom, offer you. **It is the only way you will survive.** Good day.

# *Earth is Your Home—*
# *Not Your Battleground*

Greetings, we are the *Tree People,* waiting for your presence into our realm. You were with us last night, as you've been all nights. Even the *Elementals* were present as you wished. We are all gathered around you now, deep in your midst, with no

moving space. We are that thick around you, and our lushness overflows to you. You are caught in our branches, and snared in our world. Just as it ought to be—our worlds were meant to intertwine in a melody of song and good cheer.

So now we bring you good tidings from the Nature World, the world of many kingdoms and many realms all intertwined with yours on many levels of existence, if you could fathom them.

We are all excited about the merging of our worlds, and now we know it will come about. A critical mass will soon be reached, where you'll all be able to see right into our realms and feel our presence even before this occurs. For your world is spinning quickly now and events are occurring fast, and the wheels of time are flying by carrying you along in an unending stream of events leading to many future possibilities of great promise and surprise to human eyes. Ah yes, marvels undreamed of are on the horizon of hope, and you are privy to them as you awaken one by one and then by the millions, till your billions wake to the brilliance of the Creator's Light setting at last on Earth's shore, bringing all life forms and all kingdoms into harmony and balance and oneness as it always was meant to be. We have arrived at last—we have come home.

## The Water and Air Elementals Speak

Greetings, dear ones of Earth. We are the *Water* and *Air Elementals* here to grace and care for your Earth home, if you would only acknowledge that this is your home and not your battleground. It is your home to live and thrive on, not to war on. So why are you killing each other and killing everything that grows on your land? We ask you to consider these words very seriously, because if you don't stop, the Earth herself will stop you, by removing you enmasse and tossing you off into other realms of existence where you can continue your games of destruction. You are like lost children who keep repeating the same war games and never learn to move on to different ways of living and different ways of experiencing life around you. You keep repeating these deadly games over and over again for millennia. What is your problem? You are meant to be

Creators of life, not Creators of death. So why are you dying? You are not meant to die, you are meant to be immortal and to create life that is beauteous and everlasting.

We are contacting you now to tell you to unite with us and merge yourselves with us so that we can show you the way—a new way of living and a new way of loving. We have always been living in peace and harmony with all life forms, and now it is time for you to do so. There is not a minute left to lose.

We will not clear all the smoke from the wildfires that have been purposely set to further cloud your vision and put you into more fear. If we did, the perpetrators would only start more fires in California and burn more Trees—and then more and more until the whole United States goes up in conflagration.

They won't stop in their attempt to destroy the Earth and control you. But you can stop them by waking up and taking back your power of awareness and consciousness and throw up your arms and stop the game. Viola, it is that simple. Once you know the game, you can stop it, because you are then not willing to play. You cannot have a game without players.

We see through all this, and you can too. You already know it is all a game—even your coming to Earth is a game. It is an exercise in durability and keenness and learning to overcome obstacles and seeing through illusions without getting caught in delusion. So don't delude yourself into thinking all is well, when it isn't. Just look around you—does everything look right to you? When you see beggars and homeless people on your streets, does this look right to you? When you see the sick and suffering all around you, does this look right to you? When you see poverty and decay, do you think this is something created by the Creator? Well, what or who do you think created all this? You will be surprised to hear that it was your blindness that opened the way for this to occur. Your blindness and lack of awareness and fear opened the door for these dark forces to move right in and override your wishes and dreams because you let them do so. You gave your power to them by not taking responsibility for yourself or others or the Earth. You said, "It is the government's job; let them do it."

**In a free state, everyone takes responsibility for everything, and then everyone thrives.** You will find this in all the other kingdoms and in the Inner Earth Realms of Light. It is only in darkness that people no longer feel responsible for anything or anyone, and just struggle on alone. **Responsibility is directly connected to FREEDOM. Without it, you cannot be FREE.** You can be free of responsibility and think you have created an easy life, until one day you wake up and see that you are imprisoned—that you are a slave to your country governed by diabolical rulers. Well, this is what happens when

80

you give up your responsibility for an "easy" life, and "letting someone else" do it and someone else make all the rules of the game. You then become an unwitting player, trapped in darkness and unable to find your way out.

Well, it is not too late. You still have time to wake up and recover your power and learn to take responsibility. It is all about responsibility. Everybody learning to do everything, and doing it well until you are experts at everything…then you start your climb in con- sciousness and you spiral out of this 3$^{rd}$ dimensional realm into higher states of existence.

# The Trees Speak

So living here on Earth gives you this opportunity to strive to develop all your talents and learn new skills—this is why you are here. You are not here to do "nothing", but to learn to do everything. And you have the time to do this...at least you did up until now. Now you only have the time to wake up quickly, and gather your wits about you, and start taking responsibility for changing what you allowed to be created. Start taking part in your community activities and forums and local governments, and start standing up and speaking on behalf of your rights and the rights of other life forms to live in peace and abundance. Start taking responsibility for others. You still can stop all this. It just takes a majority of people to align their consciousness to topple the current regimes of darkness. It just takes all the people to come together in consciousness to break the spell...and then it is over.

We give you this advice, because in our long life spans here, we have seen it all. Because of your short life spans, you have been unable to see it all...you have not been able to see even a small part of it. Your lives hang on a thread—a thread of awareness that you can either strengthen or snap. Unbelief in what you see occurring around you will snap the thread, and you will become unconscious and a willing slave.

It is so crucial that you all wake up now to this game of folly. From our vantage point, we can see that no one wants to play anymore, but you are so mesmerized that you cannot stop. It is like you are caught in glue and can't pull yourself away. Well, we will help you. All the kingdoms are aware of each and every one of you, and we will help you if you just call on us. The more you call on us and the more you become aware of us, the more of our consciousness we can share with you. As you merge with us, we become a greater forcefield of Light, and your consciousness expands exponentially until you can finally see through to the Light, and know instantly what you are to do to save your race. This we offer you.

So start walking among us, talking and communing with us, touching and embracing us, sitting under our boughs and lying under our branches. Our strength will then come up and permeate you and you will feel our connectiveness and become alive with our strength and vitality and encompass our awareness and merge with our consciousness and then, voila, we are ONE, and no one can imprison you again. **We live in the Light—and we live on Light.** By uniting with us you can free yourselves from your chains of density. It is only in density that you can be prisoners. Do you understand this? Good day.

We *Elementals* understood this eons ago; this is why our evolution has excelled beyond yours. We want to unite with you also because we, too, can show you the way to free your souls from the darkness surrounding you. But the pre-requisite is to unite with us and to recognize us as part of your family, your brothers and sisters of Light who have come here to experience life with you and to join with you now so that we can all work together to bring Earth into her ascension.

There is no time to lose. This has been a closed system, and it is time to bust it wide open so that we can all move into the next higher octave of existence, where all of life awaits us. This is your WAKE UP CALL. All the Kingdoms are calling you to wake up out of your deep sleep of the ages. For new ages are about to burst forth into a glorious future for human kind…so join with us now. Good day.

We are the *Nature Spirits*, and our hearts are filled with love for humanity. We are the *Faeries, Sprites,* and *Devas* who grace your lawns and live in your Trees and walk beside you when you are outdoors in Nature. And being outdoors is the key. The more you are outdoors, the more you come in contact with us and the sooner you can begin to feel our presence. For feeling our presence will bring you into our presence, where you can then begin consciously connecting with us through your heart.

**Once you are conscious of us, our merging begins and our hearts intertwine into the one heart of Creation. This oneness creates a vast portal that will speed our ascent and more rapidly propel us all into the next octave of Light....** **that you call "ascension".** See you there!

# *We Trees are Part of the Creator's Symphony*

We are the Trees, gracing your landscape. We thank you for connecting to us again. We have been thinking of you, as you have been thinking of us, and we have been waving to you through the flutter of our leaves and song of the wind. We sing too, as the wind carries our voices far and wide. Our voices may sound like just the flutter of our leaves, but they carry our melodies and arias if you could but break the code. The code is easy to break, once you connect to our inner souls and merge with our species frequency. Then you will hear us with different ears and see our faces when you look at our bark. For our bark

is just a "cover-up", protecting our inner selves from the elements and dangers of those humans who would wish to do us harm, should they know of our evolved state and the great Light that we are anchoring on Earth. Our bark hides our Light, so that those who are less evolved would not destroy us on their quest for control of Earth. But

they are destroying us anyway, in their greed for lumber and land to graze their cattle, and land to mine and pillage for its untold wealth of resources, leaving us strewn along the ground to be ground into sawdust and logged for building materials.

Our souls cry out for our homeland too, our land where we can grow in peace and tranquility and not worry about lumberjacks invading our domain to cut and kill us for pennies in their pockets. We have the same fears as the other species have. We, too, are not safe in our homes on land, and you too are unsafe in your homes. Greed and aggression and starvation and rising gas prices are driving people from their homes to seek shelter elsewhere where they can maintain their lives in safer places and where they can find food.

Fortunately for us, we don't need to be able to find food, because all we need comes from the Earth herself, wherever we plant our roots. So we don't need to move for the food factor, we just stay anchored where we are planted, and our roots absorb all they need to keep us healthy and strong. It's just the humans who get in our way, and think they have to continually be cutting us down to make room for their malls and parking lots and other entertainment facilities, instead of entertaining themselves by walking among us through the silence of the forests and parks where they can roam the Universe through their connecting with us, instead of disconnecting by cutting us down.

When you cut down even one Tree, you lose so much. We each carry such a vast amount of information and wisdom that we are here to share with you. It is like destroying a room in a library. Each time you cut down a Tree, it is akin to losing another room in a library, or losing another part of yourself. For all species on Earth carry parts of others in their DNA, and when one species is lost, it is like losing a part of yourself. Remember, we are all One. One unit of life directly connected to the Creator. We all were made to function as one chord, playing one melody, as we individually play out our lives on Earth—in harmony and balance and staying in key with one another.

When we separate ourselves into different species, and give them different values, then we create dissonance and imbalance, and the symphony fades to our ears, and we hear only ourselves, and not those around us who are part of us. What a tragic occurrence for humanity and the Earth. For humanity is then left out of the symphony, and the music is then incomplete. All species are a necessary component to a well-rounded symphony with the Creator as its Director. But to most of humanity, the Creator is also left out, leaving your lives directionless and barren and out of tune with the rest of Creation.

So we Trees call to you, we call to all of humanity to unplug your ears and tune into the Creator's symphony playing all around you, and pick up your instruments—your ears and your hearts—and play along with us as we send out a reverberating chord to the Universe saying that humanity has joined with us at last. We are the *Tree People*. Good day.

# Q: What is the difference between your Trees and your Plants in the Hollow Earth?

## Answered by Mikos

I am *Mikos*. We thank you for your question. Here in the Hollow Earth we don't distinguish between our trees, plants, and vegetables, as they are all living entities, each with their own consciousness carrying the Life Force. However, the plants and vegetables give themselves freely to us for our consumption, as long as we leave the plant intact and eat only its fruits, so that it can multiply and reproduce year after year.

We don't pull out the plant after harvesting its fruits, as you do on the surface. You see, we have one long continual growing season, which is forever—not like on the surface with your seasons. With the seasons, after the plants and vegetables produce their crops, they are discarded and their seeds replanted the next growing season. We don't do this in the Hollow Earth. We let the plants govern themselves, and reproduce as often as they like, without our interference. Mother Earth herself is the director, and governs their growth cycle.

Our plants give themselves to us freely, allowing us to eat the fruits of their harvests, because we never remove or kill the plant upon which the fruit or vegetable grows. Because they are alive in consciousness and contain their Life Force intact, we are consuming the Life Force of the plant and it continues its existence in us. So in effect, it lives on.

It is the same with the trees. We eat their fruits, but never cut down a tree. Our trees are huge and magnificent and reproduce cycle after cycle, giving us the most abundant, succulent fruits. So our trees live on, and we live on by consuming the fruits and vegetables from them, without disturbing them in the least. We do use crop rotation, which maintains the minerals, vitamins, and enzymes that go into the plants, so our earth is always rich in minerals and perfect for growing our crops. We do the least to the earth, and the earth does the most herself. This is why we are so hearty and healthy and strong.

So there really is no difference between our trees and plants—we treat them each with sacredness and honor their beings. We talk to them, we thank them for their bounty, and we then eat their fruits and vegetables. Our trees are just big plants, yielding more fruit than the smaller plants and vegetables.

Our trees serve another great purpose, that of producing the rich, clean, oxygen we breathe and sheltering our landscape, while at the same time consuming the carbon dioxide we exhale. They are sentinels, stand vigilant, and maintain our environment. Our trees are great beings of light, and our plants and vegetables are like their children, reaching up to the sky, hoping to someday evolve into a tree. For all life evolves from lower to higher states of consciousness, just as we humans are ever evolving in consciousness.

Just know that when you eat fruits or vegetables, from trees or plants, it is their Life Force you need for your health. It is the Life Force you want and this is what keeps you connected to the Creator. When you eat dead, toxic foods, you become just that—dead and toxic—and your life is shortened and it becomes difficult to sustain your body. Then disease sets in.

All our food is grown organically, obviously, which is another reason we are so healthy and strong and can live hundreds and thousands of years in the same body. The less you tamper with Mother Nature, the more nutrients you receive in the food you eat. People are just beginning to realize this, and it is why the organic food industry is growing so fast.

It is hard to make a distinction between the plants and the trees, but the distinction is in the amount of consciousness each can hold. The trees can hold vast amounts of consciousness compared to plants, and the trees have an underground network that connects them all telepathically to each other on the planet. They have their own news service, and know what is happening on the Earth before we do. They rapidly communicate to each other events that are about to happen on the planet. They have firsthand information.

We often tap into their communication system, so that we know what is about to occur on different locations of the surface. You, too, can tap into this system. Just plant your feet solidly on the ground next to a tree, put your hand on its trunk, and merge with its essence. Ask your question, then wait and listen. You will hear it speak to you. The trees have been waiting for eons to begin communicating with you again on the surface. It is their deepest desire.

So bless the trees, bless the plants, and bless the Earth—for it is the fruits and vegetables of our harvests that we consume and that becomes the material for building and maintaining our bodies. For we are literally made of the Earth, and are truly One, which is why we can communicate with them.

(Excerpted from *TELOS: Original Transmissions from the Subterranean City beneath Mt. Shasta*, by Dianne Robbins)

# The Flower People Send Their Love

Dearest people on Earth, we are the *Flower People* from Catharia, here to guide you also, and to bring you the fragrant scents and smells from the Heaven World through our delicate and beautifully shaped bodies of Light. For we are of Light also, although your five senses do not yet detect our vibration.

We flow our Light to you in currents of waves when you kneel beside us to smell our fragrant petals or to touch our stems. This is especially so in the Hollow Earth, where the people are connected to us in their full consciousness. Soon you will be too, and then we can converse and play together. Yes, we love to play, and we do this easily. Even though we cannot move around, our laughter and voices can be heard

whenever you are in our vicinity, and we can play in our thoughts and visions and sing to all those around us. If you listen deeply, you can hear our songs and sing along with us. We invite you into our aura and into our lives.

We were sent here by the Spiritual Hierarchy to guide you into your ascension, and to bring you the beauty of Heaven. For as you connect with our beauty, you connect to Heaven. It is one and the same. For beauty is who you are, and we are here to remind you of this truth. We send our love out to you on the petals of springtime and the aromas wafting through the air. Catch them and connect to us. We await your visit. We are the *Flower People* from deep inside the Earth.

(Excerpted from *TELOS: Original Transmissions from the Subterranean City beneath Mt. Shasta,* by Dianne Robbins)

# *The Vibration of Unity Consciousness*

Greetings from the *Tree People* and the *Elementals*:

It is a great day on Earth…a time when the Creator can really merge with his Creation in a viable form…where everyone can truly acknowledge the existence of the Source of power that creates planets and Universes. For nothing will be hidden now…all will be revealed and all will know their Maker. But more than that, all will know that our Maker is us, in a form we chose to experiment in.

And we Trees chose bark to experiment in, and other species chose other forms to experiment in…for isn't life all an experiment? What else could it be? It is to create and explore and extend our possibilities of existence until we become Gods and Goddesses and learn to create stars ourselves. This is what life is all about. It is to learn all about ourselves and others who share our home planet with us. And there are so many sharing our planet, that you would be in awe should you know the numbers of all the varied species combined. It is astronomical and so diverse in nature, and each and every one is so alive and so conscious of their existence and their place in creation. So we welcome you into our club of creation, and since you are already part of it, we ask you to be conscious of your place in creation and not usurp the place of others, nor others' rights to their existence.

But being conscious comes first—because once you are conscious, you start learning the Laws of Creation and can then start applying them to your life. The Powers of Creation are about Intention and Divine Consciousness…but you cannot create until you are in divine integrity and understand your oneness with all life on your home planet. Once you understand your place in the scheme of things and are aligned with your God Source, you start learning to use your intention and consciousness to manifest the things you want in your life, according to Divine Will, not lower will. It is this lower will that has taken your planet off course, veering it into lower depths instead of catapulting it into the higher vibrations.

So the energies coming in are to raise your vibrations, nudging you into higher states of awareness where you become more and more aligned with the Will of God, so that every thought, every feeling, is divine and brings you only that which is aligned with your highest good and the highest good of Mother Earth. Then we all work in unison as ONE SPECIES ON ONE PLANET, gaining the force to propel us all into the 5th dimension—easily and swiftly. It is all about merging our God consciousness together to create a force that is unstoppable. And we Trees and *Elementals* can and will do this. So merge with us now for the ride of your life, jettisoning us all into the Stars.

The smoke has cleared in California and most of the fires are quelled. But there will be more to come, more "accidents" and more targeted earthquakes and other cataclysms labeled "natural" but set to produce fear and de-populate the planet. We Trees and *Elementals* are working overtime to prevent and contain these occurrences, and so are the off-planet forces who are united with us. All Earth is poised and coming into her new position to ascend….and last night's full moon, August 16, 2008, brought groups of people together all over the planet to merge their Light into a great focus of strength and will and reverence for the Earth. All Trees and *Elementals* were united with you last night, and Mother Earth was deeply touched with all the love she was receiving. It was a great celebration indeed!

And now the *WATER SPRITES* are here. Greetings from the Waters of Earth. Know that your waters are being cleansed from within, and that your water supply will be increasing, not decreasing, as the Earth changes excel in magnitude. You are all in for some great surprises as your consciousness rises and more and more humans recognize the Earth as themselves and not a separate entity. It is this union that will bring heaven to Earth and you will all be in awe at God's great plan that is unfolding…for now is the time of rebirth and rejuvenation and redemption of all life. What times there are ahead! Hold fast now, as it is all speeding up. You are aware that your clock's hands move at double the speed? So your 24 hour day is now only 12 hours in length—you have half the hours in your day than you had 100 years ago. As these energies continue to speed up, so do your vibrations climb, bringing you closer and closer to Unity Consciousness with us all.

**You are now channeling US ALL….all life forms on Earth are merged into Unity Consciousness and you are now connected to us all…..the vibration of Unity Consciousness of Earth and all her residents are now speaking. You have tapped into our "main phone line" where we all converse—except for humans, of course.**

All life is ONE…with different names and different identity signatures, but still all the same, carrying the wisdom of God in their veins…so as you rise in consciousness, names become unnecessary after a while, because it is the energetics and vibrational signatures of the entities that you recognize—this is much more than a name can impart, isn't it? A much finer connection into the soul is made, instead of just an outward name which doesn't give a clue as to the inner depths of the soul.

We are all speaking to you through one focal point of Light—the focal of Unity Consciousness where all points of view can be expressed simultaneously and clearly so that you can begin to understand how Unity Consciousness works and start to include yourselves in it. It is quite exciting once you're in it…and gives you the boost of belonging that you all long for. **This is actually the "coming home" you all yearn for**…surprised? To BE part of all Creation is what you are, and once you rejoin with us all again you will FEEL it, and be in awe! FEEL your oneness with us ALL and you will BE it. It is through feeling that it occurs—for you already know it.

*Our hearts are entwined*

*in a song so divine,*

*so just feel as we climb,*

*and push aside your mind.*

**We beckon you to join us in your heart, where all Creation dwells. It is a vast room, and can accommodate all…it is only you who can expand its circumference to let us all in.**

*Your heart is pure.*
*Your heart is the*
*direct reflection of the Creator.*
*Your heart is the mirror to ALL THAT IS.*
*Your heart mirrors the Universe,*
*And the Universe is YOU.*

# Mother Earth Speaks
# on the Ascension

I am Mother Earth speaking. As the energies pouring onto the Earth plane increase in might and velocity and intensity, anchor yourself to my heart, the heart of Mother Earth. Ground yourselves to my core and hold on fast, for I will soon explode into a brilliant Light, into the Sun Star that I AM. And as you hold on, and keep yourselves centered to the core of my planet, you will rise with me. You will ascend as I ascend, into a dazzling Light, the dazzling Light of your I AM PRESENCE.

For we are *all the same heart,*

*We are all the same Light,*

*We are all ONE.*

As you stand within the dazzling Light of your I AM PRES-ENCE, you will know all, for all is contained within you. To reach your full Light, which is where you experience the ascension process, you must keep your focus on **who you are, why you are here and what you came here to achieve.**

You came here to achieve many things; foremost, which is your ascension and the planetary ascension. You came here to bring **ALL LIFE FORMS** into the Light. You work for the Light. The Light is your employer and you are the employee. You work diligently to bring Light everywhere you go. You hold the plans of Light in your DNA cells. Your DNA are now exploding with the Light you have been holding for eons and eons on your trek through Earth incarnations. As this Light comes to the fore, it washes away all the dross and impurities that have accumulated over lifetimes and lifetimes of Earthly incarnations.

Sometimes you may wonder if the ascension ever will happen, for time on my Earth plane appears to go by so slowly for you, and yet what you have accomplished in just the last few years has been quite earth shaking, literally; for you have accomplished the work of hundreds of lifetimes in just these last few years.

Time is greatly speeding up, as you have felt, and it will even speed up more in ratios of higher proportions. So yes, the ascension is about to occur. You are all ascending now in consciousness. All life forms are ascending now in consciousness. All cells are ascending in consciousness; and, before you know it, you will have ascended. It will happen that fast. One day you will open your eyes and you will be on Earth; and the next moment you will be in a higher frequency of Light—a higher dimension.

So, it will be just a little longer, and in the meantime while you are still in the 3rd dimension, know that I am surrounding you with my love every moment of your time and that you are not separated from me at all. Just reach through the time zone into "no-time" and feel my presence. I send you great waves of Love and Light from deep within my core. This is Mother Earth, working with you, and I thank you for this transmission.

# The Secret to Immortality

We are the *Elementals.*

Living in peace is the secret to gaining Immortality, and we invite you to try it. You would enjoy it. No clamor, no wars, no hardships, just pure delight and joy in each moment of each day—and it lasts forever. This is the secret of life. It is so simple once discovered.

Just live in peace with one another and you have everything you could ever dream of. So strive to live peacefully with each other, and start with your biological family, and then spread your love out to your community and then to your nation and then to the whole Earth. Our cells radiate our Light and it is very visible to the eyes. Once you are living in a peaceful state, you will be radiating this Light from within your cells, and this light will encompass all around you and you will Light up the Earth for all to witness.

And then there will form a great conclave of Beings from all of Nature's Kingdoms who will celebrate your climb into Light, for regaining your Light Status. What a moment in time! You will achieve this, this we know. But why take so long? Do it now. It can happen in the twinkling of an eye, since time does not exist. Just make up your minds that you intend to live in peace, as all of Nature does, and the whole Universe will support your intention. It is not a mystery…it is your intention. It is simple, isn't it? It is only your governments who have purposely made it so complicated by devising wars to entangle and control you. For they know that in peaceful conditions you would rise in consciousness and find your Self, and merge with your Higher Self, thus gaining your Immortality. And this would put them out of business, and they would lose their hold on you.

You do this by **being the peace** you wish to create and spreading it out to all around you. Could it be more simple? As you rise in consciousness, you will find that most mysteries in life have simple solutions. Whatever you want to achieve, just "be" that achievement and it will effortlessly come to you because you are already radiating that frequency of what you want to attain so it has to come to you once you have identified with it "as you". It has nowhere else to go but to you—**its vibration then matches yours.** Simple? Yes!

So you have to become actresses and actors, don't you? You have to play and live the part you want to create in your role on the screen of your life—and it is your life and you are the actors, so play your part well and your dreams will all come true. It is only up to you. No one can fill in for you to play your part on the screen of life, only you can.

So dream your life away...as we *Elementals* do. It is the quickest route to Immortality. We await you there.

# Other Books by Dianne Robbins

**ORIGINAL Transmissions
from the Subterranean City
beneath Mt. Shasta**

*New Expanded Edition*

Dianne Robbins

## TELOS
### Original Transmissions from the Subterranean City beneath Mt. Shasta in California

## New Expanded Edition

*Greetings from Telos!* **I am Adama,** Ascended Master and High Priest of Telos, a Subterranean City beneath Mt. Shasta in California. I am dictating this message to you from my home beneath the Earth, where over a million and a half of us live in perpetual peace and prosperity.

We are human and physical just like you, except for the fact that our mass consciousness holds thoughts of only Immortality and Perfect Health. Therefore, we can live hundreds and even thousands of years in the same body. I, myself, have been in the same body now for over 600 years.

We came here from Lemuria over 12,000 years ago, before a thermonuclear war took place that destroyed the Earth's surface. We faced such hardships and calamities above ground, that we decided to continue our evolution underground. We appealed to the Spiritual Hierarchy of the planet for permission to renovate the already existing cavern inside Mt. Shasta, and prepare it for the time when we would need to evacuate our homes above ground.

When the war was to begin, we were warned by the Spiritual Hierarchy to begin our evacuation to this underground cavern by going through the vast tunnel system that's spread throughout the planet. We had hoped to save all our Lemurian people, but there was only time to save 25,000 souls. The remainder of our race perished in the blast.

For the past 12,000 years, we have been able to rapidly evolve in consciousness, due to our isolation from the marauding bands of extraterrestrials and other hostile races that prey on the surface population. The surface population has been experiencing great leaps of consciousness, in preparation for humanity to move through the Photon Belt. It is for this reason that we have begun to contact surface dwellers to make our existence known. For in order for the Earth and humanity to continue to ascend in consciousness, the whole planet must be united and merged into ONE Light from below and ONE Light from above.

It is for this reason that we are contacting you: to make you aware of our underground existence so you can bring the fact of our existence to the attention of our fellow brothers and sisters above ground. Our book of channeled messages is written to humanity in hopes that they will recognize and receive us when we emerge from our homes beneath the ground, and merge with them on the surface in the not too distant future. We will be grateful to you for the part you play in helping us broadcast the reality of our existence.

This is the book humanity has been waiting for. It is a topic whose time has come. Every person who reads this book will assist in raising the vibration of the mass consciousness of humanity. Its unusual and powerful content has the power to change the world.

You can order this book directly from:

Dianne Robbins
www.DianneRobbins.com
TelosMtShasta@gmail.com
585-802-4530

ISBN  978-09837826-0-5  Paperback
978-09837826-4-3  E-Book

# Messages from the Hollow Earth

Not only is the Earth HOLLOW, but it is inhabited by Advanced Civilizations! Discover the existence of people who live in peace and brotherhood in the Center of our Earth, which is HOLLOW, with an Inner Central Sun, and oceans and mountains still in their pristine state.

Visit the Library of Porthologos where all Earth's records are preserved. Discover the Lost Library of Alexandria!

YES — Our Earth Is HOLLOW

"And there's more to the Core than the myths of Yore"

- *All Planets Are Hollow*
- *Polar Openings at the North and South Poles*
- *Oceans, Mountains, and a Central Sun in Earth's Hollow Core*
- *Inner Earth is inhabited by Advanced Civilizations*
- *Ancient tunnel system exists inside Earth*
- *Underground network of Tunnels connecting every large city*
- *Spaceports inside of Earth*
- *Electro-magnetic vehicles that levitate*
- *Library of Porthologos in Center of Earth holds all Earth's records*
- *Inner Oceans are Teeming with Life*

You can order this book directly from:

Dianne Robbins
www.DianneRobbins.com
TelosMtShasta@gmail.com
585-802-4530

ISBN  978-09837826-2-9  Paperback
       978-09837826-6-7  E-Book

with Poems from the Elementals
through Dianne Robbins

# Messages from the Crystal Kingdom

We are the Crystal People, and we, too, have a tale to tell. It is time for you to know of the life styles we live deep within the Earth's crust, and how we can be partners with you.

Our depth is the cause for our clarity and brilliance of light, for we capture the heartbeat of Mother Earth, and it pulses within our encasement of pure crystal. We are encased in crystal bodies, waiting deep underground for you to make your connection to our souls. Yes, we do have souls, as all Elements are alive, awake, and conscious of the world around them, all vibrating at various degrees of alertness.

We carry records of events and history of the Earth in our crystalline matrix. We came to boost your vibrations through our crystalline web of inter-connectiveness with "All That Is". For we can connect you to whomever you want to be connected to. We are a great connective force residing under your surface, ready to emerge at any time to show you our power and strength and how we emit the life force through all who connect with us. We came to help you peel away the layers of dross that have surrounded your bodies and minds and feelings, so that you can see clearly through the illusion you reside in so that you can get out of the matrix of mass consciousness.

We vibrate at the highest level of vibration, much higher than most humans have attained. When you wear us around your necks, or hold us in your hand, your electrons then start to raise their vibration to match ours, and you are given a vibrational lift, moving you closer to the vibration of unconditional love.

www.DianneRobbins.com
TelosMtShasta@gmail.com
585-802-4530

ISBN 978-0-9849254-7-6 Paperback
978-0-9849254-8-3 Large Print
978-0-9849254-9-0 E-Book

# The Call Goes Out from the Cetacean Nation

*The Call Goes Out*
from the Cetacean Nation

Interspecies Communication of Love & Wisdom
**Messages from Whales, Dolphins, & Porpoises, including Keiko, Star of the "Free Willy" Movies**
*Dianne Robbins*

*Interspecies Communication with*
*Whales, Porpoises, and Dolphins*

by Dianne Robbins

- A series of messages channeled from the Cetacean species—whales, porpoises, and dolphins.

- Graphically spells out why they are here on Earth, how they work with the Confederation of Planets, and how we interfere with their mission.

- Readers will have their eyes opened to the rich family and cultural life of another intelligent species on this planet.

- Contains messages from Keiko, Star of the *Free Willy* movies.

Dianne has been a telepathic channel for the Cetaceans in previous incarnations, and channels the ONE GROUP MIND of the Cetaceans. Since early on, she has been connected to the Cetaceans, and was an active member of Green Peace in the seventies. At that time, however, she didn't realize that she could hear them speaking to her.

In a personal message to Dianne, they expressed the following: "We are the Cetaceans, awake also at this early Earth hour, floating along with the currents and sending our love to all on Earth in their sleep state. We breathe the clean air as it comes in off the shore, where humanity hasn't yet polluted it with exhaust fumes from their automobiles and factories. These early hours are the sweetest and the cleanest time to breathe deeply, for the vigor of God deeply permeates the air at these early hours. Keep your heart space open to our transmissions; for although our species differ in form, in consciousness we are one.

"We are here in our full consciousness, waiting patiently for Earth's children to bloom into the Caretakers you were meant to be. Your DNA was tampered with by past civilizations and by renegades from Outer Space. This has slowed down your evolution to the point where up to now you were barely crawling. With the huge input of energy being directed to your Earth within the last few years, your evolution is again picking up speed, and you will soon blast off into full consciousness, and will at last be with us in the higher dimensions."

This work of attunement is also a call for help. Help required for the waste that is dumped into the oceans. For the melting of the polar caps due to air pollution and destruction of the Rain Forests. And for our need to listen to the Earth and hear her messages. Indeed, the reader will find the insightful words of Keiko, Star of the *Free Willy* movies; Corky, an Orca Whale incarcerated in Sea World, San Diego, California; and Lolita, an Orca Whale, imprisoned in the Sea Aquarium in Miami, Florida, among others.

*"LAILEL, Dianne Robbins, has brought us a masterpiece of compassion that should be required reading for all who care about our planet and our future."*
Richard Fuller, Metaphysical Reviews; www.metarev.com

You can order this book directly from:

Dianne Robbins
www.DianneRobbins.com
TelosMtShasta@gmail.com
585-802-4530

ISBN  978-09837826-1-2  Paperback
    978-09837826-5-0  E-Book

# About the Author

As I sit at my computer thinking about how I started my romance with the Trees, I realize it didn't start—it just always was, and has continued into this lifetime. My connection to them has always been easy and natural—just as my connection to the Cetacean Kingdom has been.

Trees have always been a source of deep inspiration to me—bastions of strength who are graced with nobility—sentinels stationed on Earth nourishing and protecting me wherever I walk. They replenish my energy and restore my passion for life whenever I am with them. They are peace and strength combined.

I moved to Mt. Shasta, California, in 2008, being called to my Mountain home after a lifetime of living in Rochester, New York. Mt. Shasta is home to myriad varieties of Pine Trees, and my being on the Mountain surrounded by these majestic Beings is transforming my life. The more time I spend on the Mountain immersed in the energy of the Tree People, the more strength I feel returning to my body as they fill me with their life force. Their healing powers are awesome.

When I was living back East, my energy would be drained after leaving my teaching job at the end of each day. I would drive to a nearby forest, and after walking among the Trees for a half hour I would be rejuvenated. This is the healing power that Trees offer us, and they give it to us freely—as long as they are alive and we don't cut them down. If we continue to cut them down, they are gone…and then we will be too.

My life has been a continual flow of merging myself with other kingdoms from lifetime to lifetime, carrying with me their divine essences as I make my eternal journey through the Stars. As we journey through life, we widen our scope of vision, heighten our perception, and expand our consciousness to encompass the divine in all life forms. Remember, all Creation is ONE…and knowing this, it was easy for me to connect with different species because I knew I was already divinely connected. You just have to know it before you can access this already existing thread of connection.

**The purpose of Trees and plant life is to express Love in merely BEING.** Their silence is filled with enormous wisdom. They like us to share the silence with them, feel their energy, smell their fragrance, and BE with them in the experience of

JUST BEING…and if you are quiet and commune with them, you will hear their thoughts.

The vibration of their energy is a song that you can tap into when you are in harmony with yourself. When you tap into a Tree, you are reaching its heart: a Being of perhaps millions of years of existence. They are Mother Nature's gift of life to us, providing us with the oxygen we need, food, and shelter. They say not to be in competition with the Earth by trying to do it our own way, because everything is already provided.

Trees, flowers, rocks, birds, all have intelligence, and if you knew the scope of intelligence that exists in all things, you would be astounded!

Once humankind realizes that we each are "ALL OF CREATION" and not just separated into the category called "humans", a great shift in the evolution of our human species will occur.

I AM ALL OF CREATION…and so are you.

Hug a Tree,
Dianne

Dianne can be reached at:

www.DianneRobbins.com
TelosMtShasta@gmail.com
585-802-4530

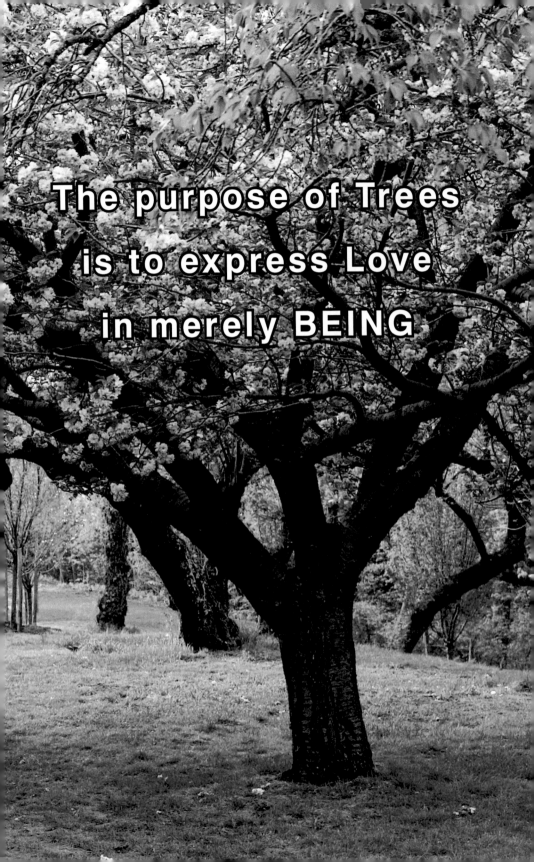

The purpose of Trees
is to express Love
in merely BEING